READ ABOUT

Gymnastics

Tim Wood

WARWICK PRESS
New York/London/Toronto/Sydney

Published in 1990 by Warwick Press,
387 Park Avenue South, New York, New York 10016.
First published in 1989 by Kingfisher Books Ltd.
Copyright © Grisewood & Dempsey Ltd. 1989.

Library of Congress Catalog Card No. 89-22550
ISBN 0-531-19072-2

Printed in Spain

Contents

If you find an unusual or difficult word in this book, check for an explanation in the glossary on pages 30 and 31.

The Competition

The crowd falls silent as Clare takes up the starting pose for her floor routine. The music begins, and Clare springs lightly across the mat doing a series of flips which end in a perfect double backward somersault. There is a roar of applause. On the other side of the hall, John is finishing his exercise on the horizontal bar. All eyes turn to the scoreboard. Will Clare and John win?

Skillful gymnasts make difficult exercises look easy. As you read this book you will find out how gymnasts build up the skills, confidence, and courage they need in order to perform well.

How it all Began

Many centuries ago, the Ancient Greeks built the first special buildings for physical exercise. These were called "gymnasia." The founder of modern gymnastics was Friedrich Jahn, a German school teacher, who opened the first open-air gymnasium in 1811. By 1896 gymnastics was a well-established sport and was included in the first modern Olympic Games in Athens, the capital city of Greece.

Traveling acrobats entertained people in China over 2,000 years ago.

The "Bull Dancers" of
Ancient Crete performed
dangerous acrobatic tricks.

During the Middle Ages,
acrobats and tumblers like
these performed at fairs and
festivals.

Modern Gymnastics

The three main branches of modern gymnastics are artistic gymnastics, rhythmic gymnastics, and sports acrobatics. Artistic gymnasts perform on pieces of apparatus. At a competition, the apparatus is set out on a large platform called a podium.

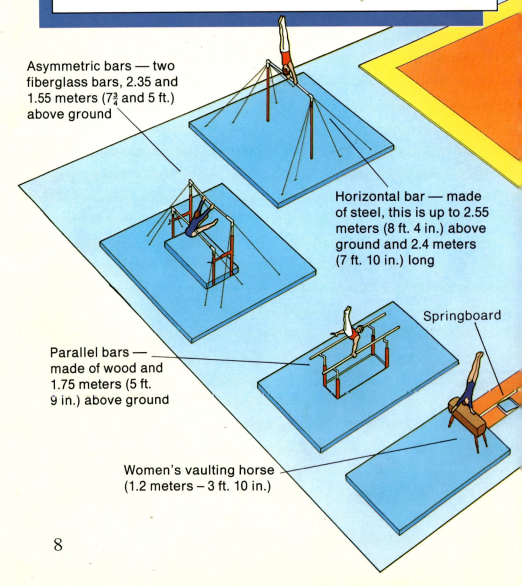

Asymmetric bars — two fiberglass bars, 2.35 and 1.55 meters (7¾ and 5 ft.) above ground

Horizontal bar — made of steel, this is up to 2.55 meters (8 ft. 4 in.) above ground and 2.4 meters (7 ft. 10 in.) long

Springboard

Parallel bars — made of wood and 1.75 meters (5 ft. 9 in.) above ground

Women's vaulting horse (1.2 meters – 3 ft. 10 in.)

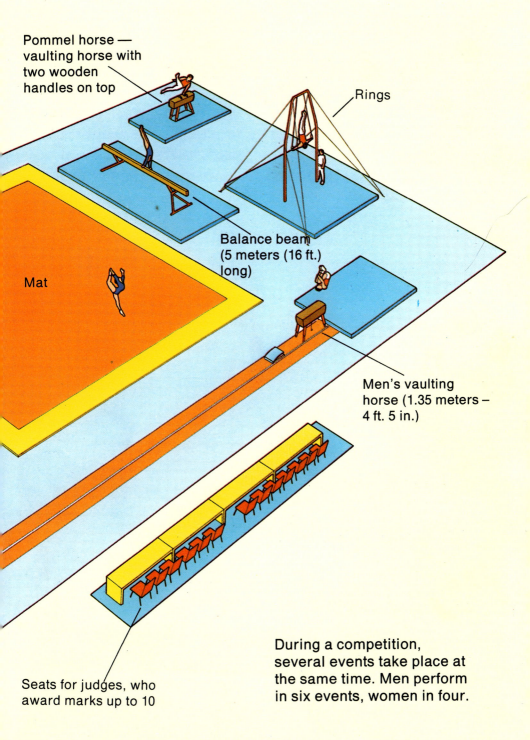

Pommel horse —
vaulting horse with
two wooden
handles on top

Rings

Balance beam
(5 meters (16 ft.)
long)

Mat

Men's vaulting
horse (1.35 meters –
4 ft. 5 in.)

Seats for judges, who
award marks up to 10

During a competition,
several events take place at
the same time. Men perform
in six events, women in four.

9

Beam and Bars

Women artistic gymnasts use four pieces of floor apparatus, including bars set at different heights and a wooden balance beam about 1 meter (3 ft.) high. The gymnast jumps up to perform on the flat top of the beam. Exercises include walking and running steps in both directions, and balances, jumps, and leaps.

The top of the beam is only 10 centimeters (4 inches) wide.

A gymnast on the beam

Asymmetric bars

Part of the routine must be on the high bar.

Gymnasts swing from bar to bar.

Part of the routine must be on the low bar.

Gymnasts must be strong and have excellent timing to perform all of the swinging and circling movements which make up asymmetric bar work.

Floor and Vault

The other two women's exercises are vault and floor. The vault calls for speed and agility. The floor exercises are done to music and contain the widest range of movements in gymnastics. During her routine, the gymnast tries to show her agility, suppleness, and acrobatic skill.

Springboard

A vaulter sprints toward the horse and uses the springboard to take off. After landing, she immediately vaults off onto the other side, in a twist or somersault movement. Two vaults are completed but only the higher mark counts.

FLOOR EXERCISE

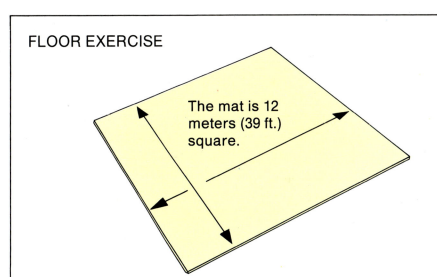

The mat is 12 meters (39 ft.) square.

The floor exercise has to contain three tumble runs which are made from corner to corner. The rest of the routine is made up of turns, balances, jumps, and leaps, linked together with dance movements. The gymnast should use the whole area of the mat.

Bars and Pommel Horse

Male artistic gymnasts perform on six pieces of apparatus. They need great strength and excellent timing to make the swinging movements that are needed for exercises on the horizontal bar, the parallel bars, and the pommel horse.

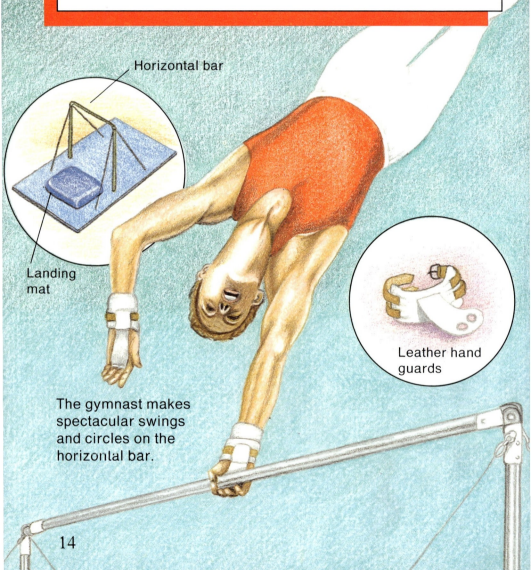

Horizontal bar

Landing mat

Leather hand guards

The gymnast makes spectacular swings and circles on the horizontal bar.

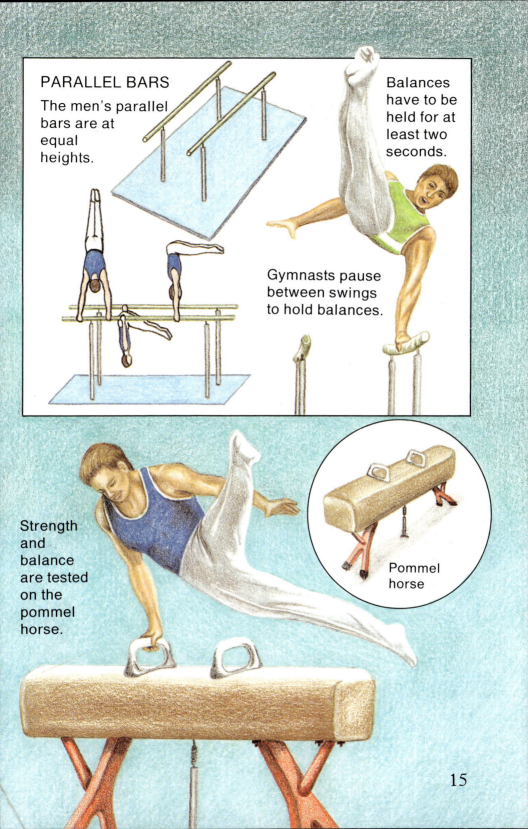

PARALLEL BARS

The men's parallel bars are at equal heights.

Balances have to be held for at least two seconds.

Gymnasts pause between swings to hold balances.

Strength and balance are tested on the pommel horse.

Pommel horse

15

Rings, Floor, and Vault

The other three pieces of apparatus used by men are the rings, the floor mat, and the vaulting horse. The floor exercise is shorter than the women's, and the men show off their agility, strength, and balance rather than their grace and suppleness.

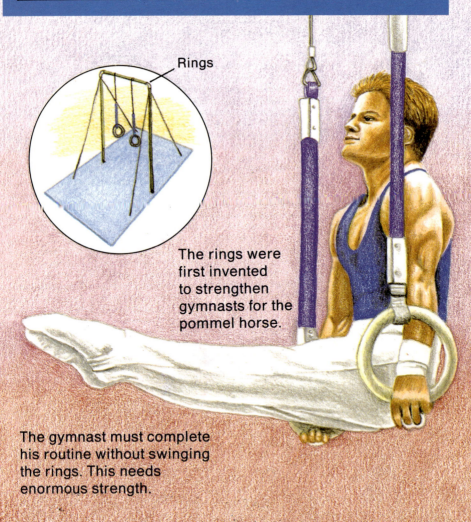

Rings

The rings were first invented to strengthen gymnasts for the pommel horse.

The gymnast must complete his routine without swinging the rings. This needs enormous strength.

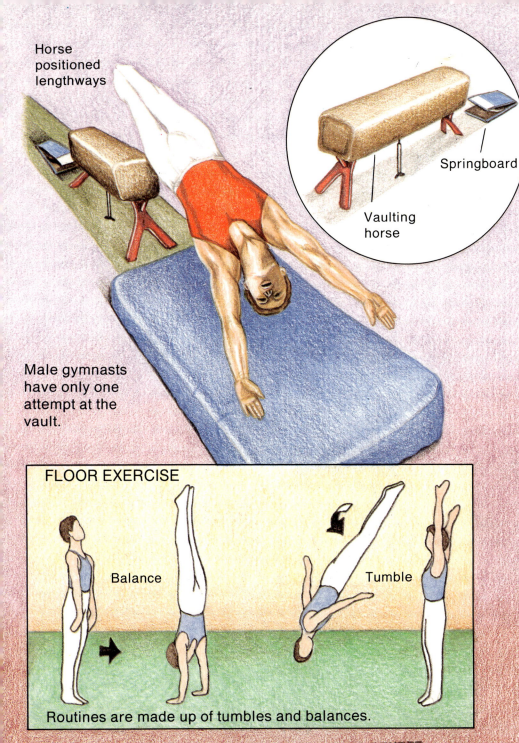

Horse positioned lengthways

Springboard

Vaulting horse

Male gymnasts have only one attempt at the vault.

FLOOR EXERCISE

Balance

Tumble

Routines are made up of tumbles and balances.

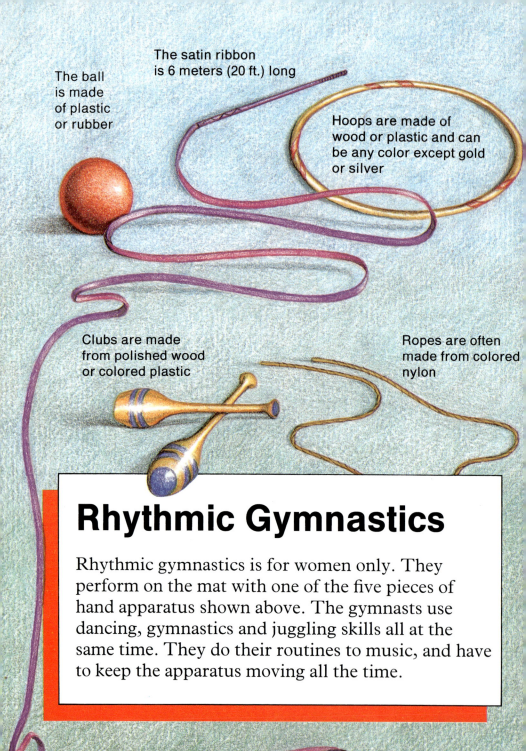

The ball is made of plastic or rubber

The satin ribbon is 6 meters (20 ft.) long

Hoops are made of wood or plastic and can be any color except gold or silver

Clubs are made from polished wood or colored plastic

Ropes are often made from colored nylon

Rhythmic Gymnastics

Rhythmic gymnastics is for women only. They perform on the mat with one of the five pieces of hand apparatus shown above. The gymnasts use dancing, gymnastics and juggling skills all at the same time. They do their routines to music, and have to keep the apparatus moving all the time.

◀ The ball is thrown in the air, or bounced. It cannot be held, but has to be balanced on the palm of the hand.

▶ The gymnast can skip or jump through the rope. It can also be thrown in the air.

▲ The two clubs are swung, twirled, and thrown in the air. They can even be bounced or rolled on the floor.

▶ The hoop can be thrown in the air, bounced, or rolled along.

Team Events

Rhythmic gymnastics can also be performed by teams of up to six women gymnasts. In team events the gymnasts can use more than one type of apparatus. The gymnasts perform with their own apparatus, but must also exchange them with other members of the team at least four times.

The twirling patterns of the ribbon create some of the most beautiful effects in rhythmic gymnastics.

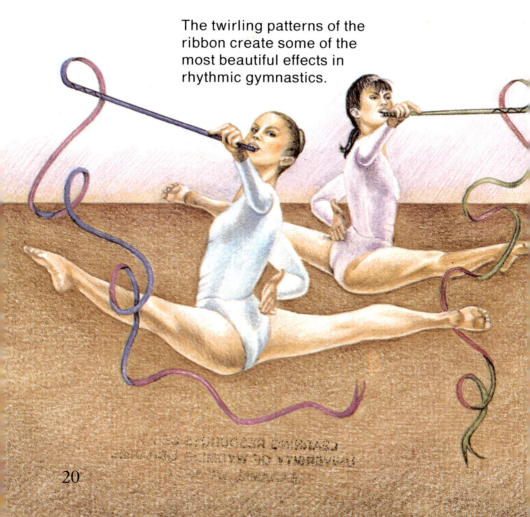

TEAM ROUTINES

Team routines last longer than individual routines, and a team of six gymnasts will perform for up to three minutes. Each exchange of apparatus must be done in a different way. During the routine, the team must make at least six different formations on the floor. The judges award marks for individual skills, for the harmony of the group work, and for the quality and originality of the choreography.

◄ A mixed pair. There are also men's and women's pairs.

► One section of the men's fours exercise is the set pyramid. Only one gymnast may have his feet on the ground.

22

Sports Acrobatics

Sports acrobatics are rather like circus performances. Solo gymnasts perform tumble runs which include double and even triple backward somersaults. Team events involve making pyramids to show the gymnasts' strength and balance, and tempo routines, in which one of the gymnasts is thrown by the other members of the team.

During the tempo, throws and somersaults are performed to music.

Routines last about three minutes.

IMPORTANT
You must never try any of these tricks or tumbles without proper safety mats or supervision by a qualified coach.

Preparing Yourself

Gymnasts need to keep their bodies in top physical shape. This is not simply a matter of doing a few exercises — diet and sleeping habits are also very important. Gymnasts should also wear neat clothing which will not interfere with their performance.

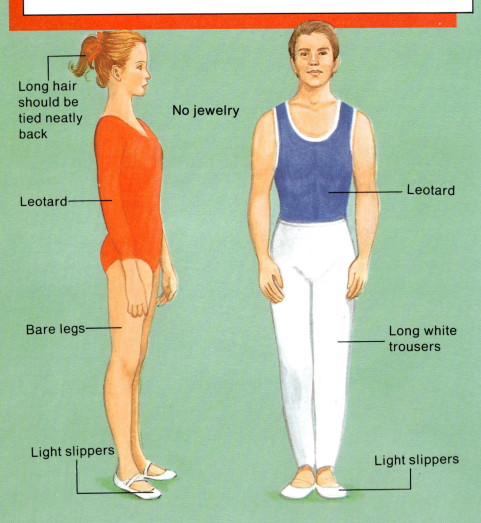

Long hair should be tied neatly back

No jewelry

Leotard

Leotard

Bare legs

Long white trousers

Light slippers

Light slippers

◀ Cut out any unhealthy eating habits. Gymnasts avoid eating too much fatty or sweet food.

▶ A sensible diet with plenty of salad, fruit, and fish help to keep gymnasts slim and fit.

WARMING UP

Warming up prevents muscle strains and tears. Try to do these simple exercises thoroughly, rather than quickly.

Gentle head rolling

Arm circling

Bending and stretching knees

Circling the ankles

Jumping on the spot

Twisting upper body

Bending upper body

Touching your toes

Be Supple – Be Strong

A gymnast needs the strength of a weight-lifter, the suppleness of a ballet dancer, and the agility of a trapeze artist. Unfortunately these skills do not come naturally, so all gymnasts need to work hard to keep their bodies in good condition. Jogging is good for all-round fitness, but special exercises are needed to develop strength and suppleness.

1

1. Sit with the soles of your feet pressed together. Press your knees down gently toward the floor.

2

2. Bend your front leg and lean your weight on to it, like a fencer lunging forward.

3. Start in a crouch. Keep your hands pressed flat on the floor and try to straighten your legs.

3

4

Hands flat on wall, back straight

4. Try to push your shoulders down as far as possible in this position.

5. Keeping your back straight and toes pointed, reach along your left leg as far as you can. Repeat with your right leg.

5

6

6. Squat down, then straighten your legs to jump as high as possible. Repeat.

7

7. Lie on your back with your legs bent. Put your arms behind your head and sit up slowly.

8.

8. Lie on your tummy. Lift your head and legs at the same time to arch your back as much as possible.

9

9. Lean against a wall and push off from it as if you were doing press-ups.

Unless you land with bent legs and straight back, you could damage your spine.

All stretching should be done slowly and gently. Make sure you avoid these two common mistakes.

In a crab, keep shoulders and knees bent to protect your spine.

Your Own Routine

You can have fun making up your own routine. You should only do this in a gym, with a properly qualified instructor to help you. Choose a piece of music which lasts between 45 seconds and one minute. Practice arm gestures, dance steps, and attractive poses in the mirror. Plan your route around the floor, using as much space as possible.

Arabesque

Full-turn jump

1. Keep your body straight and make a full-turn jump. Bend the knees to cushion the landing.

2. Try to form a shape like this, with a straight supporting leg.

28

3. Do a forward roll, keeping your back rounded. Push against the floor with your hands at the start to cushion the impact.

Cartwheel

3

4. Do a cartwheel, making a good star shape.

Forward roll

4

6. Push up from a lying position. Jump so that your feet are just behind your hands, then straighten up.

Shoulder stand

5

Front support to crouch — keep back straight

5. Do a straight upward jump with a half turn, then sit back and roll back to a shoulder stand. Use your hands to hold your hips high, as here.

6

Glossary

Acrobat
An entertainer who performs gymnastic feats, such as tumbles and balances.

Agility
The skill of moving the body, arms and feet quickly and neatly.

Apparatus
A piece of equipment used in gymnastics. Those used in artistic gymnastics, such as the horizontal bar or vaulting horse, are large and stand on the floor. The apparatus used in rhythmic gymnastics is much smaller and can be held in the hand.

Arabesque
A balance on one foot, with the other foot lifted high at the back while the body is tilted forward.

Artistic gymnastics
The main type of gymnastics, where gymnasts perform on a floor mat or on different pieces of apparatus such as the beam or rings.

Asymmetric bars
A piece of apparatus used by women. It consists of two horizontal bars, one higher than the other.

Choreography
The dance steps which are put into a gymnastic routine.

Exercise
A single movement in gymnastics.

Gymnasium
A building used for gymnastics.

Hand guard
A leather hand protector.

Horizontal bar
A high bar used in men's artistic gymnastics.

Leotard
A tight-fitting costume.

Parallel bars
A piece of apparatus used in artistic gymnastics consisting of two parallel bars set at equal heights.

Podium
A raised platform on which gymnastics events are held.

Pommel horse
A piece of apparatus used in men's artistic gymnastics.

Pyramid
A human tower made during sports acrobatics.

Rhythmic gymnastics
A branch of gymnastics in which women and girls use hand-held apparatus.

Routine
A series of exercises joined together into a single sequence to make a display.

Shoulder stand
A balance in gymnastics where the body is supported on the shoulders.

Sports acrobatics
A branch of gymnastics in which gymnasts perform acrobatics alone or in groups.

Suppleness
A wide range of movement in the joints of the body.

Tempo
Part of a routine in sports acrobatics when one of the gymnasts is thrown by the others.

Trapeze artist
A circus performer who does tricks on high swings.

Tumblers
Originally medieval acrobats and traveling performers. Now taken to mean anyone who performs acrobatics.

Tumble run
A run, often diagonally across the mat, during which a gymnast performs a series of tumbles joined together into a single routine.

Tumbling
A solo event in sports acrobatics. It includes flips, springs, and somersaults. Tumbling is also part of the floor exercises in artistic gymnastics.

Vaulting horse
A leather-covered box on legs, over which gymnasts jump using a springboard to help them take off.

Index